D1177257

SABOTAGE

Also by Emma Gannon

Nonfiction
Ctrl Alt Delete
The Multi-Hyphen Life

Fiction
Olive

SABOTAGE

HOW TO GET OUT OF YOUR OWN WAY

EMMA GANNON

Andrews McMeel
PUBLISHING®

To my fellow saboteurs

CONTENTS

INTRODUCTION

ONE GOOD THING ABOUT THE MODERN WORLD IS you can search for absolutely anything online and a few minutes later locate it, even if you're in the middle of nowhere. On a whim last year, I booked and paid for a drop-in therapist session while I was staying in a remote town by the sea to write for a week because the streets of London were suffocating me. I had rented an apartment at the top of a five-story, skinny old house with a purple front door that had a broken lock. I emailed the owner of the house gently requesting that the front door lock be fixed, to which he swiftly replied that there was "hardly any crime in this town" and I'd "be just fine." Let's just say that that response didn't help with my anxiety, so I drank wine every night and sprayed the strongest lavender spray I owned on my pillow in order to fall asleep. I was also getting up each day at 6 a.m. to finish the painful last drafts of my first novel—a novel I hadn't sold yet. It was an old house, but it had a comfy bed of soft white linen, big white square pillows, and views of the sea (albeit gray). I was having a hard time with the book; my imposter syndrome was stomping around and breaking things like that giant creature in the film *Colossal*. Who did I think I was, trying to write a novel anyway? Why had I taken time off from my paid job to try this? Why should I bother? What if people laugh at me? What if I got rejected? What if it was terrible? Negative thoughts replayed on a loop.

Despite everything on paper seeming "good" from the outside, I wasn't feeling good. I was feeling like no amount of achievement would ever matter, because deep down my self-worth was the same as that nine-year-old girl on the playground who had been the last to be picked in the sports team and last to be picked by any group of friends. I could tell my struggles were jarring for other people. They'd scratch their head and say, "But why aren't you happier? Look at what you have." They had a point. Why couldn't I be a "normal" person and just be happy? It's disconcerting and exhausting when how you perceive yourself contrasts so aggressively with how others perceive you—and I felt like I was dragging myself down unnecessarily. If opening your palms to the sky means welcoming things in, my palms were scrunched up into tiny, tight balls of fear.

I have always been skeptical of life coaches, therapists, and healers. I was once scammed in a basement "clinic" (read: someone's ramshackle apartment) in New York where an eighty-year-old woman told me I looked "gray" and needed more "sparkle" in my life. She sold me some "energy sprinkles" for $100 and told me I should put them in my bed, under my pillow, and they would heal me. When I got home, I realized she had sold me a small packet of . . . confetti. So yeah, I've been made a fool of before and have been wary ever since. But this session I'd booked from the rented house by the sea had come via a friend's recommendation, so that made me feel more at ease.

Her name was Lulu and she was wearing MC Hammer pants. I went into her home-slash-clinic, lay down on the massage table type of bed in her living room, and she began her work. She wasn't a straight-up talk therapy person, but she talked to me while doing some Reiki work with me. I closed my eyes and started thinking about my weekly shopping list. After some long minutes, my brain finally chilled out and started drifting into an imageless cloud of relaxation. My mind went black. Then I started feeling vibrations over my whole body, and it felt slightly uncomfortable. She had her eyes closed, her hands hovering over my chest, and she said:

"You want big things."

"Mhmm," I murmured back, nodding very slightly.

"You want it, but you're blocking it."

"I am?" I asked quietly.

"You don't believe in yourself," she said softly.

"Mm."

"Things could be huge for you, Emma. But you really have to get out of your way."

Her words rang in my ears, and I closed my eyes, having a sudden flashback. A vivid colorful memory began playing in front of me. There's me at ten, in art class. I'm wearing a navy-blue apron and wild hair. I'm painting. My tongue is slightly poking out with concentration. I accidentally make a small splotch on the painting. It's small, but I know it is there. Instead of painting over it and moving on, I paint an even bigger splotch in the middle of the painting to make sure it is well and truly ruined. I ruin it the first time by accident, but I ruin it the second time on purpose. *"It's ruined,"* I say, throwing up my hands. My art teacher looks at me and sees right through what I've just done. "Oh, Emma. There's no need to do that, sweetheart."

Life is full of challenges—mostly external ones. When we leave our front door every morning, we don't know what we'll run up against. Other people and situations can sabotage our day, even when we're doing everything right:

Someone might spill their coffee on us; a flight might be canceled last minute; we might receive an unexpected bill that throws our budget off; we might not get the job we wanted because of prejudice, discrimination, or bad treatment. The world is not a meritocracy, and the world is certainly not fair. Each of us is in a roulette game of privilege and luck, with some talent and hard work also sprinkled in. Less talented people become more successful than better-skilled, harder-working people all the time. It's one big, random merry-go-round of Who Knows. As clinical psychologist Dr. Soph says, "No amount of breathing exercises is going to change the societal structures that cause the pain in the first place (such as racism, patriarchy, poverty, and other forms of pressure and oppression)."

But while there are so many things outside of our control, there is one thing we can control, and that is our relationship with ourselves. We can control the foundations we set, the choices we make, the things we do or do not do. We can choose not to self-sabotage in a world that can sabotage so much for no reason. I recently saw an artist share (on Instagram) a painting that he had ruined with a dark splotch by mistake and how he had turned the dark smudge into a spot on a Dalmatian dog. It was beautiful. It reminds me of the Stoics—how the obstacle often isn't *in* the way but in fact it *is* the way. That seems like a good place to start at least. If we help ourselves, it's one less

thing to struggle against. We can be our own worst enemy
or our own best supporter. I was talking about my self-sabotage with a friend recently and how I've slowly started
to overcome these bad habits, and she said, "You should
write about this. We all do it."

So, I put pen to paper and wrote the first few hundred words
of an essay, which was published by The Pound Project,
a small independent press that supports and crowdfunds
one writer's work at a time. The essay resonated, and I
adapted it into an online class with Skillshare about how
self-sabotaging tendencies tend to crop up when we're being
creative or putting ourselves out there. But self-sabotage
isn't just about the art we create or don't create. The project
manager I was working with on the set told me that what
I was saying about self-sabotage in creative work really
echoed what she was going through in her dating life.
The motivation behind not starting that project because
you're worried it won't work out is exactly the same as not
bothering to go on that date because you're convinced you'll
be rejected. We love to *assume* things won't work before
even giving it a go—trying to avoid throwing ourselves into
the scary unknown. In many ways, our behavior in work
and personal life mirror each other. Maybe you turn down
big job opportunities because you're dealing with imposter
syndrome. Maybe you didn't go on a second date because

he/she actually seemed pretty great—maybe in your mind too good for you. I almost sabotaged my relationship with my soon-to-be husband eight years ago. The minute things got good was the minute my brain told me to get the hell away from it all. It was like my brain said, "Uh oh, you're getting very happy and it might not last! So let's GET OUT QUICK!" I had to literally train myself to stop running away from good things. I had to realize that good things were supposed to be scary sometimes. That life is about feeling things deeply. It's not always about riding it out, waiting for things to pass, but actually being present in the moment itself.

This is not a book that is supposed to make you feel guilty or encourage self-blame—quite the opposite. We are not solely responsible for the way the world treats us or for what we get in return for our efforts. But it is a reminder that in our unpredictable, imperfect, sometimes magical world, we are responsible for our own selves and how we move within it. We can be our own cheerleader when we may need one the most. Recognizing self-sabotage is not the same as self-blame. We are not "wrong" or broken. It is simply about taking a look at the areas of our lives where we might be holding ourselves back and making small changes if we want to.

This is a book to encourage you, more than anything, to be your own resource. To need less outside validation and reassurance, which, because it doesn't come from within, often doesn't stick, leaving us at square one. Instead, how can we look inward, be able to sit alone with ourselves, and self-soothe when we need to? Of course we need friends, community, family (especially in our increasingly individualistic culture), but I think it can be a wonderful gift to yourself to feel that you are your own number-one fan. In my session with Lulu, she pointed at my chest and said, "You have everything you need right here to keep you going, to keep the fire burning. It is an endless resource." It made me realize that while I can reach out and ask for help sometimes, I can also make my own fuel, keep myself alight, and keep myself going.

This is also a book for anyone who is scared to fall in love with their life, even though you know you have a life worth loving. It's a book encouraging us all to crack ourselves open and allow ourselves to be braver and more vulnerable.

So, I hope you enjoy this book. I hope that together we can stop getting in our own way. That we can learn and want to feel all the emotions of life. That we can get to know and love ourselves better and more deeply. That we can fully experience the highs and lows and everything in between. Let's taste it all.

"I HOPE I LET MY DREAMS COME TRUE"

THIS WAS ONE OF THOSE TWEETS, WRITTEN BY FRIEND and writer Ashley C. Ford, that is so simple and powerful that you stop and stare at it for a while. It caught my eye one sunny afternoon when I was lying on my bed, and it snapped me right to attention. When it comes to wanting the things we want, it's not just as simple as hoping our dreams miraculously come true. They don't just slip through the mail slot, like those "manifest your money" scams that promise cash windfalls landing on your doorstep if you just visualize hard enough. We have to be active in the process. Life coaches often speak of "letting things in" when we're scared and have our walls up. We have to also do the work in order to allow our dreams the space to come true in the first place—the part that is often left out, the actual hard work of believing you are allowed to have good things and opening yourself up to them rather than closing yourself off. It doesn't always come naturally, to inherently believe you are deserving of something good.

"Sabotage" sounds like a strong word, but it's a useful way of framing the unhelpful daily thought patterns and quieter habits that hold us back. People often describe it as "reaching for the stars by shooting yourself in the foot" or "burning your own house to the ground." But it's not always as dramatic as that. It can be subtle. It can be done over a long stretch of time, so that it becomes invisible to the naked eye—to ourselves or to our friends. It's not a condition with a diagnosis and cut-and-dried cure. It is not about a self-help guru waving a magic wand over your head or someone telling you you're "wrong." Self-sabotage is one of the most human self-defense mechanisms. Ridding yourself of sabotaging behaviors is simply about putting yourself in a position where you are *allowing* your dreams to come true by taking the time to identify what they are in the first place and becoming an active participant in welcoming things in, instead of freaking out at the sight of them. It is about not shrinking away from your dreams out of fear. You are worthy of goodness. You are allowed to be in love with your life.

No one warned me that *that* was the tricky part in all of this.

WHAT IS SELF-SABOTAGE?

IF SELF-SABOTAGE WERE A PERSON, IT WOULD BE THAT person who, uninvited to the party, turns up anyway with muddy shoes and no snacks. Self-sabotage is a trickster who loves messing up other people's plans and constantly tells us we can't or we shouldn't. Self-sabotage loves sticking its nose in, and it needs to butt out. Self-sabotage, quite simply, gets in the way.

But this isn't actually a totally fair description of self-sabotage, because sabotaging behavior is actually us trying desperately to protect ourselves from getting hurt— it's a maladaptive way we try to care for ourselves. If I was going to make up an analogy, I'd say sabotage is like an overprotective parent who keeps their kids inside and suffocates their choices in order to keep them away from danger,

3

when really the best thing to do is to let them get out there, get hurt, and learn how to pick themselves up.

Self-sabotaging thoughts can be hard to spot, especially if it's just the way you normally speak to yourself. Adult life is so fast-paced that we don't often sit down and have a word with ourselves. Ask: Can I be kinder to myself? Can I show myself the same compassion I have for the people I love? Is that a fair self-criticism? Am I doing what I can right now?

Sabotage is the voice that tells you to drink a bottle of wine the night before a big interview because you "probably won't get it anyway." Sabotage is the voice telling you not to start that new side hustle because "it probably won't be any good and other people would do it better." Sabotage is the voice that tells you to pick a fight with your partner without explaining how you're feeling because "they probably won't understand."

Clinical neuropsychologist Judy Ho says that self-sabotage behaviors can be split into four different "LIFE" categories:

L: Low self-esteem (and therefore thinking you don't deserve good things)

I: Internalized beliefs (and finding it hard to shake them)

F: Fear of the unknown (and self-protection)

E: Excessive need for control (and preferring control over just about anything else)

Self-sabotage can be smaller, everyday things. Need to hand in a piece of work? You'll do it right after you've vacuumed the house and tidied the sock drawer. Thinking about having a serious conversation with a friend? You'll get to it right after you've watched *Friends* on Netflix. Procrastination can be a way of coping, but when it gets out of control it can be an easy way to sabotage a task that in reality wouldn't take you very long at all (more on procrastination later in the book). Sabotage is not always the big, drastic *dun-dun-dun* moments—it can be smaller, more mundane obstacles too. If anything, these are the instances we need to watch more closely, as they can slip through the net. It's the myriad ways we distract ourselves and procrastinate every day that take us away from our true feelings and intentions and further away from who we actually want to be.

Self-sabotage, sadly, seems to crop up a lot in my life. I have always had a strange urge to mess things up when they are going well. It's something I've noticed but never really accepted. I realized that I never truly let myself enjoy the good things. I always felt like any success I had might be short-lived, or on borrowed time. I would notice myself saying it out loud in conversations and then think, *Why am I so negative*? Someone would casually say "Oh, I saw that thing you worked on the other day—looked fun!" And I'd reply with, "Well, y'know, things are good for now, but who knows how long it will last!"

5

I would go home and not really know why I said it. I went through a phase of trying to preempt my own (to me, inevitable) failure so that it wouldn't hurt as much if it happened. But there is no point doing that. It's impossible to know the future and fearing future failure strips you of all your joy in the present moment. Find things that ground you and try not to hold on too tightly to things you cannot control.

I notice people who don't do this and feel in total awe of their ability to simply say "THANK YOU!" when someone compliments their work. This book really is how I was able to become more like that person who could accept when things were going well. I remember reading an interview between Russell T Davies and Phoebe Waller-Bridge in the *Guardian* and being so impressed with how she just owned the good stuff.

Russell T Davies, writer and producer: *Your success is phenomenal, and an inspiration. But no one ever teaches you how to deal with success. So . . . how's it going?*

Phoebe Waller-Bridge, writer and actor: *It's going bloody great, Russell! Thanks for saying that. Last year has been insane. I've loved every part of it. [. . .] I'm always asking myself "how would I feel if this went away" about various aspects of it all. I think the things I'd be truly gutted to lose are my creative freedom, my collaborators and a couple of really nice coats. Anything else is just a perk. One of the best of them is meeting people whose work you love.*

We might not all write award-winning TV shows, but every one of us can own our successes when they're pointed out to us. It's also infectious. When you watch someone own their successes, you feel compelled to do the same. Therefore, by being positive about yourself, you are probably inspiring someone else in the process.

SELF-SABOTAGE CAN ACTUALLY BE USEFUL

SELF-SABOTAGE IS NOT INHERENTLY "BAD." THESE feelings we get, these waves of emotion, while sometimes negative, can—if we pay attention—guide us. It helps to have compassion for ourselves in our self-sabotage moments. As life coach and cofounder of Project Love Selina Barker says: "It's so important for us to have compassion for that part of us that always seems to want to come in and mess things up, just as things are going well—whether we're daring to follow a dream or that dream finally seems to be coming true." If we take the time to understand and even forgive our self-sabotaging impulses, we can use that knowledge to move us closer toward the people we want to be. If we can redirect our negative emotions, we can change our stories.

Many things I've done are because I've wanted to prove someone wrong, and in that respect, envy doesn't sabotage my success but actually fuels it. Using a negative feeling for our own good is a way to reclaim our own power. Author Daisy Buchanan put it this way: "When we feel envious of someone, we incorrectly feel as though they are making a statement about being better than us. [But] even if we start a creative project as an act of retaliation, a sort of proof against our own inadequacies, a howl of protest against being excluded from the club, the work often ends up absorbing us and distracting ourselves from our feelings—curing the condition that inspired it in the first place. I believe that anyone who is ambitious and creative has to accept the fact that you'll have to pass through tunnels of envy as you move through your professional life. It's dark and scary and horrible—but you can't go under, you can't go over, you've got to go through! The more uncomfortable it feels, the more it has to teach you."

The older I get, the more I realize there really are clues in all of our emotions. Happiness is not a state of being that we can just permanently achieve, so having the tools to unpick the low moments allows us to find meaning in them, even if they rob us of happiness for a while.

As comedian Russell Brand said, "Don't see self-sabotage as a negative thing. See it as an inner voice waiting to be heard. There is wisdom in this information." There is wisdom to be found in just about anything.

SABOTAGING YOURSELF TO APPEAR SMALLER AND THEREFORE MORE "LIKABLE"

I USED TO FEEL LIKE I COULD NEVER SHARE MY GOOD moments with other people because I feared it would make me seem braggy or annoying. I felt like the more confident I was, the more unlikable I became.

Historically, women have been deemed more "likable" when we keep ourselves to ourselves and don't take up much room. "Wow, she loves herself" is usually said with a sneer, when actually it should be "Wow! She loves herself!" Self-sabotage and imposter syndrome really do sit side by side, and it is often a gendered problem. It is women, especially, who believe that shrinking themselves publicly will make us seem "nicer" and more digestible to others, which, in our sexist society, is often true. But I started to get sick of my own bullshit, bored of my own insecurities.

I gave myself a social experiment: *Try not putting yourself down in front of others for as long as you can*. Not shrinking yourself down makes you more of an honest person with the people around you—and is a good test of others too. If you have a "friend" who looks subtly pained or disappointed every time you share a piece of good news, it is a red flag. Friendship doesn't mean treading on eggshells trying to make yourself more palatable for those who don't like seeing you flourish.

According to a study by American Community Survey, breadwinning women still do more around the house even when they are the top household earner, whereas bread-winning men aren't expected to do anything on top of their compensated work. Women have been socially trained to always do more and always keep the people around them happy, even if they lose themselves in the process.

I asked clinical psychologist Dr. Jessamy Hibberd what she thought about this (she had just finished writing a new book called *The Imposter Cure*). Why do women have such a hard time sharing their achievements, and why do we want to be liked so much? She explained:

> "It can feel boastful or that you're bragging if you tell others about success, and if the other person isn't doing something similar, we can end up feeling bad that they don't have the same

opportunities. Because you can empathize, you can imagine that they might be upset. However, in these situations we're perhaps over-empathizing with the other person. We had to get along in a group to survive so we have a deep need for social inclusion—we feel rewarded by positive social interaction and hurt by negative interactions. That need for a sense of belonging is still part of us now and relationships are still key to our health and happiness. To succeed, humans had to be self-aware."

I found this so reassuring. Even if this behavior is linked back to millennia of social conditioning, we will not be cast out of real friendships for openly talking about our achievements, and if that does happen, then I think it's fair to say those were not your true friends. Every time we share a happy moment with our friends—a job success, a relationship milestone—we are trying to bond with our community. We don't need to be so sensitive or read too much into it. We're allowed to share our lives with others, the good and the bad and the ugly. Otherwise, we might drift through our lives never truly connecting. You might turn a few people off by opening yourself up, but it's worth it for the people you truly connect with.

Nerves, worries, fears—they make us human and they cannot be erased overnight. The weird thing about feeling like we are huge imposters about to be "outed" at any time is that these feelings can affect even the most successful of us. As Emma Watson once said: "It's almost like the better I do, the more my feeling of inadequacy actually increases." In the sports world, self-sabotage is called "choking"—it's when an accomplished athlete, with years of proven experience, suddenly starts to underperform. You don't have to be an athlete to relate to this. I find it bizarre how much I worry and stress about things that I used do so easily and breezily when I was younger. In my twenties, I wouldn't get nervous before a talk, but now I do, even though through practice and experience I am now heaps better at public speaking. This is one of the most frustrating elements of self-sabotage—I can't see any logistical reason as to why I do it.

I often feel like it's my duty as an "empowered feminist" to feel like I am an invincible superhero every single day, and if I'm not, then I'm a failure. But the truth is, some days I just don't feel invincible. And that's OK. But I also want to take logistical steps to try to quiet the voice that says I can't or I shouldn't.

THAT FRIEND, AS BRITNEY WOULD SAY, IS TOXIC

Sometimes self-sabotage can show up in whom we choose to surround ourselves with. According to motivational speaker Jim Rohn: "You are the average of the five people you spend the most time with." People often say that if you look at your friends, you're actually looking at your future. If something's not right in your friendship setup and things feel like more of a duty than a reciprocal relationship, it can be difficult to confront.

Sometimes it's not as simple as just cutting someone off, especially if you've been friends for years. But other people can sabotage your happiness, and by letting them back in time and time again, you are sabotaging yourself! Sometimes when things are going well, and an old "friend" tries to get back in touch (who you know was always a bad influence and made you feel small), it's easy to end up getting hurt again. I like living my life with a "trust everyone until they give you a reason not to" approach, but it can get exhausting to be betrayed repeatedly. As Einstein is often attributed as saying: "The definition of insanity is doing the same thing over and over again and expecting a different result." Sometimes, we have to look at the cold, hard facts of how someone makes you feel no matter how much you want to believe that "next time it'll be different."

I had a friend a few years ago who was a bit of a whirlwind romance. She was someone I'd met through work who on first impression seemed great. I did find it slightly strange that she didn't seem to have any other friends but seemingly had a lot of people she had recently fallen out with. At the time, I didn't see this as a red flag at all—if anything, it made me like her more and think these people she'd fallen out with sounded awful. They were clearly terrible friends, and they had left a good egg (her) behind. I felt lucky to be her friend, enamored by her charm, charisma, and general enthusiasm toward the same things as me. Over time, I'd notice small emotional pinpricks, which grew into small bruises from how she treated me. But one thing I found almost invisible was how she put me down very subtly, so subtly that I would often miss it:

"I really don't like that lipstick color you're wearing! But somehow you made it look OK!"

"I'd be worried if I was you about that talk you're doing, but you will totally smash it."

"I wouldn't bother submitting to that agent. She's very picky."

15

These comments would on first glance seem "support-ive," like she was "looking out for me" by being brutally honest. She made it seem like it was actually a kind thing to point out how I shouldn't bother trying certain things because she didn't want me to be upset when they didn't work out. As this behavior and the subtle digs became less subtle, I ended up even more solicitous toward her. I'd text her more often to ask after her, wondering what she must be going through to be acting the way she was toward me. I would buy her flowers when she got good news, and I would message her regularly when she said she was feeling down and then not hear back for days. I can clearly see now that she was sabotaging my happiness and confidence, and I was unwittingly letting her—because I believed in the friendship. Looking back, her advice was not in my best interest, and it brought out all my insecu-rities rather than building me up to reach for the things I wanted. Of course, no two people are ever perfect, and in any separation, there is no angel or devil, and my behavior was far from flawless. But our relationship was not healthy for me and it needed to end. If you feel someone in your life is holding you back, even subtly, it needs addressing. To keep people around who make you feel bad is a type of self-sabotage. We're told to be mindful of what we con-sume and let into our lives, and that includes the friends we let in.

HOW TO SPOT THE SIGNS OF
A TOXIC RELATIONSHIP:

- You are scared to tell them good news and may even hide good news from them.
- When you do tell them good news, they say they're pleased but actually look quite pained.
- They try to hold you back from trying new things.
- You feel yourself becoming less and less confident around them.

TIPS TO SLAY YOUR SABOTAGE:

1. Track whether you feel energized or deflated after social engagements. What made you feel good? What made you feel bad? What made you feel strange?
2. Unpick these feelings and think about what may have triggered you. Is something internal going on or did a conversation or someone else's behavior toward you leave you feeling fragile?
3. Write down the things you can control (your reactions and actions) and the things you can't control (other people's behavior toward you).
4. Ask five of your closest friends and family members to name one thing they love about you.

5. Write them down on a piece of paper or Post-it Note and put it somewhere private, like inside your wallet. These are the things that are true. And keeping them close to you means you do not need to hunt for validation elsewhere.
6. Practice sharing your good news with other people.
7. Stop yourself if you're about to sabotage a compliment. Repeat the person's words in your head and take them in. Even if you don't believe them in the moment, by accepting them and not batting them away, you are retraining your brain to start believing them.

PREEMPTING YOUR OWN REJECTION

"PREPARING FOR THE WORST" HAS BEEN PR'D INTO
being an unalloyed good. Yes, it's good to pack a raincoat
when it might rain, or a spare USB stick for a big presen-
tation at work. But while we can prepare for a lot of things,
we can't prepare for everything. We are often tricked into
thinking that if we constantly plan for the absolute worst,
then the rug can never be pulled from under us. Wrong.
We can fantasize all day about how things might go horren-
dously wrong, but my imagined outcomes have never been
exactly correct. I might have prepared myself for a certain
type of "worst-case" scenario, but the truth is, dreadful stuff
usually comes out of the blue. On a random Tuesday afternoon. We can try to prepare all we like, but all it really does
is take away our ability to feel joy in the present moment.

I learned a new word for imagining worst-case scenarios all the time—it's called "rehearsing." It's when your brain rehearses, in full emotional detail, something you are scared might happen. For example, a loved one dying.

I recently spoke to Anna Mathur, a psychotherapist who specializes in helping clients with worry and anxiety, about this:

> "I remember lying in bed one night, and my husband who works in London (which is a good hour-and-a-half commute from where we live) . . . was *really* late, and I couldn't get hold of him on the phone; he wasn't answering his text messages. So I lay there in bed, my three kids are asleep, and I just remember going through this entire scenario in my mind: Well, obviously there's been a terrorist attack and he's been killed and how the heck am I going to tell my children? Am I going to have to move back in with my parents? Should the kids come to the funeral? And I started feeling absolutely devastated. It was like I was feeling some of that grief. I was projecting my entire life and self into a future that hadn't even happened and I was feeling some of what I might have felt. What we do in those moments is we kid ourselves that should that

worst-case scenario happen, we'd be able to go, 'I knew this would happen! I have prepared myself!' We try and protect ourselves from the pain. All this does is make *now* a pretty painful and rubbish experience, when it doesn't need to be, and might never be. It just robs you of your now."

After talking to Anna, it really blew my mind how obvious and self-defeating this defense mechanism is—that by rehearsing we are not doing anything other than making our present moment miserable and making ourselves experience pain for no reason.

"WELL, I DIDN'T WANT IT THAT MUCH ANYWAY"

Sometimes we want something so much, it feels safer to mess it up. I wanted a boyfriend so badly when I was an awkward teenager that every time I came across anyone I fancied, I would blurt out the most bizarre thing or do something highly unattractive. I once burped so loudly when a boy I fancied started talking to me that he ran away and never spoke to me again. When I was nineteen, I wanted to nail my university coursework, so I would stay up for twenty-four hours on Red Bull and then end up ill in bed for a week. When I was twenty-two, I fell in love and was terrified of being happy, so tried to push him away. When I was twenty-four, I wanted to write a book so badly that I went to a book event, got drunk on overpriced gin and tonics, live-tweeted horrible things about the evening, and pissed off the entire panel. It's sometimes easier to sabotage our path so we have something to blame our failure on and convince ourselves that *we didn't want it anyway!* If we mess up almost on purpose, we have an excuse for failing before we even get close to reaching a dream goal.

We think we're being so clever by sabotaging ourselves before anyone else can! The brilliant clinical psychologist Dr. Soph, who specializes in overcoming insecurities, put it this way: "If you fear you are unlovable and not enough, you may be so sure that you will be rejected that you start preempting the rejection. You may look for all the reasons the relationship won't work; you may start testing the other person or pushing them away. You may decide to take control and reject the other person quickly, as this is safer than getting further down the line when you are more invested and then they reject you." It's as though we are looking for that confirmation of our existing bias. It's almost as if we find what we are looking for, if we search hard enough. So why not change what we're searching for, and maybe find different things?

We would rather be in control, even if that means ruining something—a relationship, project, opportunity—

rather than not know how things are going to turn out. If you do a crappy job on something, then you know the outcome—it will be crappy! But there's a risk too that if you pour your heart and soul and best efforts into a creative project, you may still be told you're not very good. But we all know that the real rich goodness of life comes from taking that risk. Sometimes we need to risk feeling hurt, rejected, or left out, for the magic that might be awaiting us on the other side.

Just like I ruined my fixable painting with a big splotch of paint, we don't need to mess up first in order to preempt failure. Take the risk, invest the effort, be present in your own life.

TIPS TO SLAY YOUR SABOTAGE:

1. If you are feeling like you are "rehearsing" often or finding yourself in a repetitive loop, it can help to write down your thoughts. When you write them down, you can immediately see where you might be exaggerating or catastrophizing. Often, when we write down our anxious thoughts, we can more clearly see them as illogical, whereas when they drift around in our heads, we can rationalize them more easily. Get them down onto a page, read them out loud, notice which bits don't seem true or helpful, and then rip up the paper.

2. Try observing your thoughts as if from an outside perspective, or as if you were a third party. Brené Brown often suggests using the phrases "the story I'm making up is" or "I'm having the thought that" to help get you out of your own head. This allows you to distance yourself from your thoughts, gently analyzing them instead of getting caught in a repetitive loop.

3. Move. If you're finding yourself having the same repetitive worry, then it can help to move location, or even move your body in a different way. When we stay in the same position physically—for example, in bed or in the same room—we can more easily get stuck in a cycle. We often need a change of location to help trigger a change of mindset. Go for a walk, look around you, shift gears.

SOME SABOTAGE-Y THINGS I AM PERSONALLY WORKING ON:

- Being constantly late.
- Staying up too late.
- Leaving things until the last minute.
- Undervaluing myself and my work.
- Snapping at my partner when I'm actually in need of support.
- Not saying how I really feel.

- Using "self-care" as an excuse not to do something that fundamentally would be good or challenging or interesting.
- Talking myself out of things.
- Avoiding replying to emails that would literally take two minutes to respond to.
- Getting a bit too drunk the night before an important early morning meeting.
- Saying yes when I mean no.
- Sleeping in when I have a deadline.
- Pushing away friends when I'm feeling down.
- Splurging on expensive things as a lazy pick-me-up.
- Replying to a message or email that has bothered me very quickly and snappily without taking the time to properly reflect (sleep on it!).
- Reading horrible comments!
- Reading horrible Amazon reviews!
- Scrolling endlessly and pointlessly through my phone right before bed with the bright blue light that keeps me up in my face.
- Wearing a white t-shirt before eating spaghetti Bolognese.
- Talking myself out of exercising despite knowing deep down that I quite enjoy it once I'm doing it.

DISTRACTING
OURSELVES TO DEATH

"But do you know how old I will be by
the time I learn to really play the piano /
act / paint / write a decent play?"

"Yes . . . the same age you will be if you don't."
— Julia Cameron, *The Artist's Way*

BEING DISTRACTED STOPS US FROM RECOGNIZING
what is holding us back. And we live in a world chock-
full of distraction. We reach for our phone when we don't
want to think about something. Or a glass of wine. Or a
night out, or sleeping too much, or too little. Anything
to not have to think about our problems. Having feelings
is an essential part of being human, but actually *feeling*
our feelings can be difficult. For so long I would numb
my feelings by drinking and constantly scrolling through
other people's lives on social media, keeping me from ever

digging deep to properly understand what was going on in my own. I could just push down any questions or feelings of inadequacy, pretend they weren't there. It's extremely hard to look our issues in the eye—and it's becoming harder living in a world of technology and targeted advertising. It often feels like the world doesn't want us to deal with our own inner issues—because then they wouldn't make as much money off us. It's much easier to watch something, listen to something, or buy something than to look in the mirror for an uncomfortable moment. Sitting with our thoughts is often not fun at all.

One of the top distractions, of course, is social media. For me, I often turn to social media when I get anxious, but spending too much time on social media makes me more anxious still. It is a never-ending loop, looking for comfort in the very place that exacerbates the bad feelings I had in the first place. It's difficult to get out of any cycle, habit, or routine. Especially so on social media, as the apps themselves have been designed in such a way to keep us there.

Social media also breeds comparison ("the thief of joy," as the saying goes). We all have self-sabotage triggers, those things that make us think things like "Why do I bother," "They're more talented than me," or "My idea probably isn't even that good." When we scroll through social media, we are opening ourselves up to so many external triggers that can come at us at a bad time. We might be just about to start a new creative side project and see an Instagram post reminding us that we are worried about money. Or that someone else has just launched a similar idea. Or anything that makes us feel inadequate—maybe someone with more money, or more followers, or more accolades. Even if it is illogical to compare, sometimes it's just too tempting, and it sabotages our motivation.

Author Nir Eyal says that we can put our foot down when it comes to these companies trying to constantly distract us. He calls it "the hack back." Social media companies have a vested interest in trying to hack our brains, but we can do something about it. Making a pact with ourselves can be very encouraging. Giving a talk at the United Kingdom's RSA (Royal Society for the encouragement of Arts, Manufactures and Commerce), Eyal gave an example of how he wanted to stop staying up late and being tired the next day, so he installed a software program that turned off his internet router at 10 p.m. every night. Could he turn it back on? Yes. But did he? Most of the time no, because the software had interrupted his pattern, which was enough to send him off to bed. What little hacks can we add to our own lives to stop us from being distracted for too long? I have gotten into a habit of emailing myself messages like "Stop refreshing your emails and do some writing now." There's no shame in leaving yourself little online breadcrumbs to stay on track.

It's easier to fall into distraction, but the rewards of self-knowledge, mindfulness, and emotional literacy are vast. Feeling our feelings is hugely important. During difficult times I have been known to go on what I call "a sad run." It means going for a jog around the park, sunglasses on (even if it's not sunny), and feeling all my sadness. Sometimes I'll help the sadness along by listening to a sad song. The point is, I'll dedicate an hour to just fully feeling sad, feeling the depths of my emotions, and not trying to feel better, just feeling what I need to feel, without distraction. During a sad run I'm not trying to feel better necessarily; I'm trying to lean into the feelings, and feel them properly. The process of self-discovery and growth can be uncomfortable, but it's worth it.

PAUSE BEFORE YOU REPLY

The upside of being so connected online is exactly that, feeling connected. The downside is that it's a never-ending source of distraction, and it can be enable some of our worst impulses if we let it.

Author Marie Forleo once joked that she won't touch Twitter after even just one glass of wine. We laughed, but she meant it—it's not worth the chance of slippery fingers when you could reach so many people. Why would you risk sabotaging years of hard work by accidentally saying something you might regret in the morning?

A friend and I recently went to a countryside retreat together just outside of London. She had just finished a huge project and she needed a few days off, so we booked something and hopped on a train. We stayed in a barn with two bedrooms and two baths and a log fire. We read books, we watched crappy TV, we enjoyed hearing the noises outside: birds, rain, farming equipment. At around 9 p.m., a storm hit and the lights in the barn went out, so we reached for the flashlights and went outside to look up at the thunderous sky. I texted the owners saying the electric had gone. They replied, "Yes, it happens. This isn't London, I'm afraid." I loved it there. Things occasionally broke because of nature and no one cared.

The next day, we had breakfast outside with the sunshine on our faces. As I chewed on a piece of fruit, I reached for my phone, and I saw a passive-aggressive tweet directed at me. Someone had made a horrible comment about me and decided to kindly tag me in it. I replied straight away, retweeting it to my followers, saying something sarcastic about how much I love it when people tag me in negative reviews of my work!

My friend came outside, holding a jug of orange juice, and sat down beside me.

"What's happened?" she asked. "I can sense an energy shift." (She's not even joking when she says things like this.)

"I'm fine. I just saw a horrible tweet, and now I feel worse because I replied to it."

"I once read that you shouldn't reply to *anything* if you have that stressed-out current running through your body. When you're typing from a place of being riled up, you will never say what you truly wanted to say. It's always best to wait 'til you have simmered and then decide if you even care about replying."

Sometimes I get annoyed with how good her advice can be. I took it on board, across social media and emails, and it's been pretty life-changing. I've lowered the chances of sabotage, just by sleeping on it. (Or at least, putting it down, going for a breath of fresh air, and coming back to it later.)

COMPARISON IS THE THIEF OF JOY

The concept of "Shine Theory," coined by podcasters and authors Aminatou Sow and Ann Friedman, is the practice of mutual investment with the simple premise that "I don't shine if you don't shine [. . .] a commitment to collaborating with rather than competing against other people—especially other women." I believe deeply in Shine Theory.

However, there is no denying that sometimes it's hard to put into practice. Sometimes you see someone succeeding in something you want to succeed in, and you feel something horrible and rotten. You feel yourself get hot, bothered, tetchy, sad, jealous, like something is being taken away from you. Like someone has reached into your life and stolen the very thing you wanted. It takes a long time to practice keeping your eyes on your own paper. But as online consultant Sara Tasker says: "Nothing blows you off track like watching somebody else's work more closely than you watch your own."

A few years ago, I became preoccupied with a woman in my industry who was doing things similar to me. I hate to admit it, but I followed her religiously and it was bordering on obsessive. I would start every day by looking at her profile first thing in the morning. Now I look back and realize, of course, that was basically setting myself up for failure and bad energy before I'd even gotten out of bed! Everything I did I compared with her. I felt like I couldn't be proud of my achievements even if they felt really special because there was someone else out there doing "better." She sold more books than me. Sold more tickets to events than me. Wore more expensive clothes than me. Had more followers than me. It was just so tempting to look at my work and then directly compare it with hers and feel deflated. I had to seriously refigure this comparison in my head, because it really didn't make any sense. We were doing different things; our writing was different; we, as people, were fundamentally different. By taking her piece of the pie, she was not directly taking mine. It took hard work, but I was able to change my perspective and break my unhealthy comparison habit. My life is infinitely better for it.

Comparison is another distraction from reaching our own goals. I find it super interesting how my own painful pangs of envy tell me all the information I need to know about what I clearly feel is missing. I used to feel it when someone else got a book deal. Or when someone had just gotten engaged. I wanted those things. Some find it incredibly painful when a pregnancy announcement is posted, because they want it. For me, I don't feel envy at pregnancy, and that's an interesting thing for me to make note of too. Envy can tell us what we want—but what does our lack of envy also tell us?

I definitely used to roll my eyes when someone would say, "It's not the winning that counts; it's the taking part." I remember from a young age wanting to win. Why did so many grown-ups try to tell me it didn't matter? Of course it matters. If it didn't matter, I thought, then why do badges and trophies and certificates exist? Winning, surely, is everything.

As you grow up, you do realize there is a more nuanced meaning to what it means "to win." From the outside, we don't really know if someone is "winning." They might have a bigger house than you but be struggling in other parts of their life. Someone might have more money than you but might have inherited it and feel undeserving. You might feel someone is better looking than you—that doesn't mean that person is happy with their looks. Everyone's dreams and goals—and struggles—are different. It's important to define your own parameters for what you think success is. If you build the race track yourself and you put the finish line of success where *you* want it to be, you get to win all through your life.

When I interviewed one of my favorite writers, Seth Godin, in the early days of my podcast, he said: "I am not here to win; I am here to contribute," and it's stayed with me ever since. Shine is not finite; there's enough shine for everyone.

TIPS TO SLAY YOUR SABOTAGE:

1. There will always be someone, somewhere doing "better" than you in terms of traditional success and numbers. It is a fact. So, you might as well just let it go.
2. It is impossible to truly compare two people. You can only compare the outer layers. You are comparing two people who started in different places and who will end up in different places. Who is "ahead" or "behind" during the middle bit does not matter.

3. You don't have to use traditional metrics to define success. You get to make those up yourself. Do you want to work different hours? Do you want more travel in your job? Do you want to spend more time on your own or with family? If you determine what you are working toward, you can feel like you are in your own lane, and therefore anyone else's metric of success doesn't matter. It is true that there is "room for all of us." There is room for everyone to win.

4. Collaborate. Collaborating feels good; it's good for our overall well-being. I feel better in my mind and body when I am lifting others up. I feel more loving, fulfilled, better at my job, and happier overall. I feel more connected to the world.

5. Imperfect meditation. Take ten minutes to sit and observe how you feel. You don't need to sit cross-legged and feel "Zen"—just observe your thoughts without judgment.

6. Let it out. Instead of quieting a feeling, write it down, or put on some music and have a good cry. Better out than in.

7. If you find yourself in an unhealthy rut, look for "hacks" that will force you to change things up. Always checking social media first thing in the morning before you start your day? Try putting your phone in another room before you go to bed. If you find yourself refreshing someone's page, add a Wi-Fi block for a few hours.

8. Feel your feelings. Allow yourself to be present and aware even of uncomfortable or negative emotions. Our feelings are clues to our desires and true selves. You might be surprised about what you learn.

DON'T IGNORE YOUR INNER CONFLICT

"When I [. . .] start plotting a revenge narrative,
I know it's more likely I'm vulnerable, not
really angry. The problem is, we weren't
raised to get curious about emotions—
and it creates unnecessary conflict."

—Brené Brown

ONE WAY WE SELF-SABOTAGE OURSELVES IS WANTING
so badly for our lives to look good on the outside that we
don't pay enough attention to the inside. We can receive
outside validation for things that aren't our own version
of success and stick with them because we feel guilty for
wanting more. Like a "dream job" that plenty of other people
would die for but you find unfulfilling or a relationship that
looks "goals" when it's not. We can end up having a mismatch between our outside and our inner emotions—and
it can create emotional conflict. Sometimes our sabotage is

really trying to shake us out of old ways of thinking because we're on the wrong path.

Dr. Soph says, "One reason we may self-sabotage is because there is a mismatch between what we think we want and what we actually want. For example, I often see people who have believed they want something so badly for so long but don't seem to be putting themselves in the right position for the thing to occur. When we explore what has been happening and what it would mean if they did achieve the goal they have, it suddenly becomes clear that their goal was never theirs in the first place but was something they were told they should have or do. For example, a certain kind of relationship, 2.4 children, a certain kind of job or lifestyle."

I spoke to author Paulette Perhach, who wrote a viral essay, "A Story of a Fuck Off Fund," which was read and shared millions of times. She talked about her own experience of self-sabotage, which came from not confronting what she actually wanted because she was too focused instead on what people wanted from her. "My self-sabotage moment was trying to look successful after the 'Fuck Off Fund' happened (because I was feeling so damn successful) only to realize the financial success wasn't matching up with the renown. I just moved from the hippest neighborhood in the city to an island an hour away, where my rent is one-third of the price. My novel writing is now going great. If we're not in a place to be vulnerable enough to ask for help, then we won't get it, and we won't succeed. If we have too much ego around the material possessions of success, but they hold us back from doing the actual work, we'll spend all our energy keeping up the facade." Keeping up any sort of facade can be really exhausting, sapping the energy we need for figuring out what actually makes us feel content day-to-day.

This clash can often become a confusing rabbit hole of sabotage. We don't mean to do it, we are not sabotaging on purpose, but we perhaps haven't stripped back the layers to work out what we even want in the first place. If we can't pinpoint why we keep self-sabotaging ourselves, it might be because we haven't reflected on whether we are living the life we truly want, even if it looks very shiny on paper or to other people.

We often find it easier to block out what we really want because acknowledging our desires makes them real, and we become frightened that we may never achieve them. Or that if we do, it still won't be "enough." By living out someone else's definition of "success" (your past self's, your parents', your teachers') you are going against your natural flow. So, how do we resolve that conflict?

Deep down, we all know what we want. Sometimes, we look for it in the wrong places. Instant gratification— from Tinder to Venmo to next-day delivery—is the norm in our modern society. So, it's understandable why we expect quick fixes for bigger things in our lives as well. But quick fixes don't get at the root of our problems. It's like taping over the cracks instead of repairing the foundation. Ultimately, it is up to each of us to do the work. We hold all the secrets and energy and gut feelings and intuition, and even if we pay $500 an hour for a career coach, at the end of the day, figuring out our desires and our own definition of success starts and ends with us. We can't expect someone else to have the key to our very specific lock.

RECONNECTING WITH OUR CHILDLIKE SELVES

"What do you want to be when you grow up?" is such a weird, intense thing to ask a kid. Adults should know better, really, especially because we can often find variations on this question awkward to answer ourselves. I'm sure most seniors would shrug their shoulders and say, "I still don't know what I want to be when I grow up!" Perhaps it is a thoughtless attempt at small talk, like discussing the weather, but it can feel way too heavy. No one wants to predict their future on the spot; no one wants to be asked where they see themselves in five years, much less how they're going to spend their entire adulthood. Definitely not when you're a kid. And most of us are still just kids wearing adult clothes and wandering around doing adult things.

I have memories of being around ten years old and a teacher asking me this question. *What do you want to be when you grow up?* I just felt stupid and blurted out something random like "I dunno, a vet?" (I had no interest in biology) and exited the conversation as quickly as I could. The thing is, though, even at a young age, we actually *do* start having a strong sense of what we enjoy, but it's not as simple as turning that into a job description. It's a lot more subtle, bubbling away under the surface, and takes quieter, focused moments to identify our skills and interests. We have to look for the clues, the small meaningful moments and feelings of achievement, not just the big, loud trophy cabinet ones.

Many parts of our personality are already formed by the age of seven. As children, we are in many ways our most free and undiluted—we are creative, we are open-minded, we ask "why" a lot. If we look back to the things we were attracted to when we were young, maybe we can remember what makes us feel alive in adulthood. Did you love pulling things apart and putting them back together again? Did you come alive in drama class? Did you like building things with your hands? Did you make collages? Were you obsessed with computers? Did you enjoy working by yourself? Were you happiest when leading a group task? In which lessons, with whom, at what part of the day were you thriving the most?

It reminded me of a teacher whom I bumped into as an adult who told me I had "too many opinions" in her classes. She was laughing while saying it, a lighthearted joke perhaps, but it pointed to a truth. My career now is as a writer and columnist, where I am literally paid to have and share my opinions.

Looking back, there were so many clues in my childhood about my later career. It wasn't that I was always writing, but I do remember being happy while doing it and getting good feedback on it. One vivid memory is of one of my babysitters, who would draw a picture with some crayons and then task me with writing a story that could go along with it. Once she drew a dragon inside a house and then I scribbled four pages in my bad handwriting about an orphaned dragon who was trying to find a new family. Sometimes we ignore the clues right in front of us.

It makes me sad to think that so many of us lose touch with our creative childlike selves. These clues that pop out loudly when we are younger can so often be ignored by teachers, parents, even ourselves, because life is busy and noisy. We are taught to fall in with the crowd, follow the same old career advice, and stick to the same old path. But it doesn't have to be that way. My task to you now, reading this, is to sit down with a pen and paper and remind yourself of all the things you loved to do as a kid. It might not be the case that you will get to "quit your job and follow your dreams"—we all know things don't happen that way overnight—but even the act of reminding yourself of what you enjoy and what you are good at can lead to a new hobby or a new side hustle and a new sense of fulfillment. It can lead us back to ourselves. It can remind us who we are again.

You shouldn't ignore your inner child, so don't ignore those inner feelings of conflict. Just like any conflict, it very rarely just disappears magically on its own.

WHAT ARE YOU AFRAID OF?

In 1880, Theodore Roosevelt wrote to his brother, "My happiness is so great that it makes me almost afraid." It is terrifying to be happy—and it's terrifying to go out of our way to change things. Another way we sabotage ourselves is by staying too comfortable in what feels familiar. Ignoring any negative thoughts. Batting away any signs that something's off. It can be comforting to stay in a situation when you have become very used to what you know—a job that isn't bad enough to leave, a relationship that is "fine."

Philosopher Alain de Botton believes a lot of our fears are rooted in our younger selves and the behaviors we got used to in our childhood. Imposter syndrome can stem from your younger self always thinking an adult knows more than you, so as a grown-up you get used to thinking other people "know better" and discounting your own knowledge and abilities. We can cling to unhealthy norms, and if we were slightly anxious or sad as a child, those emotions can strangely become comforting to us, the feelings we fall back on. They might not feel good, but they can feel "normal." De Botton says: "We may prefer to choose what's comfortingly familiar even if it's difficult over what is alienatingly fulfilling or good. Getting what we want can feel unbearably risky. It puts us at the mercy of fate—it opens us up to hope and subsequent possibility of loss. Self-sabotage may make us sad but at least safely, blessedly in control."

As Dr. Soph says: "We love feeling in control. Like failure was on our own terms. I cannot tell you how often I hear people say it's better to not try because at least then if I don't succeed, that was my choice, rather than I tried and it still wasn't enough. The fear of failure is so prevalent. Few of us are taught how to fail from a young age. Few of us are taught that it is important to get it wrong from time to time, as this is how we grow and learn new skills. Not trying, procrastinating, keeps some of us feeling safe. It helps us flee our fears in the short term (the fear of failure). The problem is that avoiding short-term pain ensures we never get long-term gain."

I used to have classic childhood fears. Monsters under the bed. Someone in my closet. My imagination would run wild. We learned about Egyptian mummies at school and I'm telling you I did not sleep properly for *weeks*. I would read a *Goosebumps* book and stay awake all night thinking of ghostly shrunken heads. I used to think fear was inherently bad, that I should try to banish it. That I should be "fearLESS." That I would be a better human if I could ctrl+alt+delete fear forever. But I could never seem to do it.

Then, inspired by *Big Magic* by Elizabeth Gilbert, I accepted that you are supposed to be fearful. We are meant to have fear because fear protects us. I have been asked so many times in interviews, "When was the last time you were FEARLESS?" But I don't want to be fearless. If I were fearless, I would probably not look both ways when I crossed the road; I would, as Elizabeth Gilbert says, "have something very important missing" between my eyes. Fearless people are psychopaths. So, I have come to embrace fear. Fear can come along for the ride, but it's not allowed to get in the way.

The last time I was really scared emotionally was when I was turning down projects to give myself the time to write my first novel. Things were going well with my broadcasting and consulting career, and I had started to become comfortable. Safe. Working on things that did not light me up creatively but paid well. I was longing for that feeling that I believed being a writer was all about—taking professional risks. I had a conversation with my literary agent about trying to write a novel. Taking this on would mean writing, without telling anyone else about it, for a year. It would mean sacrificing my time for a project that might not ever be sold. It was about trying something new that might well fail. Someone had asked me what "success" would mean to me. Deep in my chest, I knew it was publishing a novel. That it was something I had never done before seemed frightening, like I was about to put my heart inside a blender. One weekend, I went to stay with my parents, and I decided to get started. I have a print on the wall of my childhood bedroom that says, "Ssh, I'm working on my novel," and it had tormented me for years. I opened my laptop, clueless, and started typing. I was starting a draft. Then I started to feel really weird. I pulled on my coat and scarf and went for a walk, pacing around the back streets of where I grew up. I felt like I had regressed, like I was back to being my teenage self. I felt small. Useless. I walked past a small park in front of an old friend's house where we used to wear Nirvana t-shirts and drink cider and pierce each other's ears with safety pins. I reached for my phone in my pocket and I called my agent.

"I don't want to write the novel anymore."

I got off the phone and burst into tears. I had lied. I was pushing away the thing I wanted most, because it made me afraid, and now I was lying to people about what I wanted to make it go away. Then I felt even worse. Going against the grain felt so wrong. It was like fear had hijacked my brain and body. It had totally taken over, and I felt like I was observing myself from outside of my body, wondering what the hell I was doing.

Self-sabotage comes from a place of fear. In this case, my fear of rejection. I simply did not want to take the chance of getting severely hurt. I was not operating from a place of love or openness. I was closing all my true feelings down.

The author Dr. Margaret Paul calls this "the ego-wounded self." This part of our self gets activated by feelings of fear and essentially tries to protect us from getting hurt or upset. It's like having our own very personal "fight or flight" coordinator. She says: "You might find yourself fleeing a work or relationship situation, or engaging in some other self-protective/self-sabotaging behavior, as if there is a real physical threat, when in reality the threat is coming from your false beliefs."

Of course, my situation was not a "big" one in the grand scheme of things—being too scared to start writing a novel because you're scared your worst creative fears will be exposed is not The End Of The World. But pretending I didn't want to be a writer, which was the *only* thing I wanted, was a clear-cut case of self-sabotage.

TURNS OUT WE ARE NOT JUST SCARED OF FAILURE, WE ARE SCARED OF OUR OWN POTENTIAL

I love to learn new words. Learning the word for a concept or behavior makes me feel like I can contain it, label it, get to know it. I recently learned the phrase "Upper Limiting," or the idea that each of us has a set limit of how much success and happiness we feel we deserve. The phrase was coined by author Gay Hendricks in *The Big Leap*: "Each of us has an inner thermostat setting that determines how much love, success, and creativity we allow ourselves to enjoy. When we exceed our inner thermostat setting, we will often do something to sabotage ourselves, causing us to drop back into the old, familiar zone where we feel secure."

If we go over that threshold, we try to scramble back to safety. It's like we hit a ceiling of how much goodness we can let in and then become petrified of aiming for anything higher. Marie Forleo calls it "our success comfort zone." She said that in her own life when things are going really well for her, she sometimes gets ill. Medical test results would always come back negative; on paper there was nothing wrong with her. She started to realize that it was like her body didn't know how to handle these scary moments of success.

This concept has stuck with me, and I've started to be more alert to it. Anytime something good happens, anytime I get a big piece of positive news, or a dream of mine looks like it is starting to come true, I'm now on the lookout for any self-sabotaging behavior. It's usually lurking, waiting to come out. Now, I make sure I swat that behavior like a fly whenever it crops up.

When we are out of our comfort zones and doing brave things, we often get scared. You might reach a huge milestone and then afterward do something extreme to make yourself come back down to earth, like overdrink, overspend, not take care of your health, start a fight with your partner. It's normal for a bad decision to follow the big high. A self-inflicted anticlimax.

We really do make things complicated for ourselves, don't we? Self-sabotage can often happen when we feel like something is "too good to be true," another shape-shifting version of fear. We have to let the fear in, because it is impossible to just get rid of it. Sabotage wants us to ignore fear, never face up to it. But we must say hello to it. Welcome it in but make it clear that it won't be running the show.

Like envy, we can also find useful information within feelings of fear. Feeling scared often means we are on to something meaningful. People always used to say to me, "It's not worth publishing unless you're a little bit scared," which I never used to understand. Now I do understand: A little bit of fear keeps us on our toes. It means we are moving forward and not staying stagnant. It's possible for us to change our relationship with fear, or even adjust the lens through which we view it, and realize feeling fearful might mean you really want something. It might just mean you're on the right track.

TIPS TO SLAY YOUR SABOTAGE:

1. If you can, work more pauses in your life. When we have quieter breaks to reflect (e.g., eating lunch without looking at your phone, going for a walk without listening to a podcast), you have more of a chance of tapping into the inner nudges and gut feelings that direct you subtly toward what you want.

2. Start journaling. Write down when you have moments of high energy and low energy. After a month, look back through for clues as to what is draining you or holding you back.

3. Take your time when making decisions. If you are someone who texts back quickly or makes up your mind on the spot, try to sit with questions longer before making any decisions. It is amazing what you can learn about yourself by taking a little more time to weigh how you would like to spend your time without the constant noise and distraction.

4. Honor your inner child. Make a list of things you enjoyed as a kid. Look for ways that you might adapt those things in your adult life.

5. Allow yourself to feel fear—it's a sign that you're taking a risk, putting yourself out there in some way. You can't be brave if you're not sometimes afraid.

FOUR COMMON TYPES OF SELF-SABOTAGE

WHILE RESEARCHING FOR THIS BOOK, I SENT OUT A
question in my newsletter asking, "Do you think you
self-sabotage? If so, how?" Hundreds of people responded,
and every single answer fit very neatly into one of four
categories:

1. PERFECTIONISM
Saying "I'm such a perfectionist" has turned into a bit of a
cliché. Like the thing people say in a job interview when
asked about their biggest weakness, a subtle humblebrag.
But as you may know, if you actually do struggle with
perfectionist tendencies, it can be quite debilitating
and stop you from finishing or even starting things.
Perfectionism isn't always wanting other people to think

you're perfect; it's more of a never-ending competition you have with yourself—believing you could be endlessly better. It can be paralyzing. For creatives, it can manifest as anxiety that stops you from making and releasing the art you want to make. Sometimes, it comes from being overpraised for academic success when you were younger, making you feel like "being smart" was a defining trait of your personality, one you *must* live up to. Or you may have experienced a really memorable, maybe traumatic, criticism from making a mistake, and you want to avoid that sort of criticism again.

I have many modes of self-sabotage, including a loud inner critic (which we'll come to below), but I seem to be the opposite of a perfectionist. I almost wish I could strike some sort of balance. But what I've realized is that some of my most interesting opportunities have come from throwing something at the wall and seeing what sticks. For example, I self-published a short essay about some ideas I had been having about my own self-sabotage, which I wrote on a very tight deadline. I was able to put out that imperfect piece in one form, and then from the reception of that essay came the opportunity to flesh my ideas out further and adapt them into this book you're reading now.

My looser creative process is why I love the format of blogging or tweeting or newslettering—because it allows you to have a space that doesn't feel as permanent as other art forms, like, for example, a novel. To a reader, a novel feels "finished" and finessed by the time it comes out, but for authors who are perfectionists, reaching an "end" can be difficult. A friend of mine recently messaged me, saying, "I'm doing the final edits on my book, and I feel like I'm now making it worse." This is a sign you are done with a project: when you start to feel like you are un-doing the work by "perfecting it" over and over again.

As Nora Ephron once said, "You don't really have to believe what you write in a blog for more than the moment when you're writing it. You don't bring the same solemnity that you would bring to an actual essay. You don't think, 'Is this what I *really* want to say?' You think, 'This is what I feel like saying at *this* moment.'"

Even though this applies to writing, which is my job, I think it's helpful to remember for all kinds of work that things don't need to be perfectly formed to matter. It's almost worth unpicking what the word "perfect" even means. If it's "absolute, complete," I think we get to decide what "complete" means to us. Anne Lamott's book *Bird by Bird* explores her creative process, which is all about breaking things down and working on questions or tasks bit by bit. It's about taking one thing at a time and not getting overloaded by the bigger picture. She says, "Perfectionism is the voice of the oppressor, the enemy of the people. It will keep you cramped and insane your whole life." For example, if you want to write a book, don't worry about writing a masterpiece; you must simply start *somewhere*. Author Dani Shapiro famously tells herself, "I will write a short bad book" every time she sits down to write. Over time, each short bad book turns into something else. For Dani Shapiro, lots of bestsellers.

Katherine Dixon, 27, English literature researcher

"As a small child, I was disqualified from a coloring-in competition because the judges wouldn't accept that a three-year-old could have stayed so closely within the lines. It is safe to say that I have always been a perfectionist. The exceptionally high standards I impose upon myself are certainly a double-edged sword. They have motivated me to strive for the moments of success I have achieved so far and, perhaps more importantly, mean that I am extremely self-reflexive. The more negative spin on this would be that I am extremely self-critical, which can also prevent me from accepting, broadcasting, or enjoying my accomplishments. At times it has been paralyzing; I have mentally written myself out of an opportunity in the belief it was beyond me before even giving it a go. Over the years, I have become more and more aware of the fact that I am the only person in the world who expects as much from me as I do, and I definitely don't expect the same standards in others. There is always a brief to be met. Sometimes you just about meet it, which is totally fine. Other times you reinvent the wheel with a cherry on top. It's for you to judge when a task demands your everything and, most of the time, it just doesn't."

TIP: Lower your expectations. Try sending an imperfect piece of work to a friend, or colleague, or stranger. Once you do it, and the world doesn't explode, it'll be easier to get your work out there.

2. PROCRASTINATION

Procrastinating is something I've done since I was a child. My most uttered phrases are "in a minute" or "not right now," used from when my mother would ask me to tidy my room to when my partner asks me to do something around the house. I am always coming up with excuses in my personal life, and in my professional life too. I don't usually procrastinate on the bigger tasks I have, biting little chunks off day by day, but I procrastinate like hell over the smaller things on my to-do list. For example, doing financial admin, replying to a nice email, booking an appointment—things that would actually only take a matter of minutes—and yet I tend to draw them out and put them off to my own detriment.

One of the most relatable things I've ever read was in Lizzie Skurnick's *That Should Be a Word:*

> "We are in dire need of a word for the email you put off responding to because you want to give your full attention and thus never answer— giving the sender the impression you don't care, when in fact it is the most important thing in your inbox."

Antonina Mamzenko, 39, photographer

> "I visualize self-sabotage as retreating into my own shell, closing the door, and hiding from everyone and everything, while at the same time longing for the world outside that shell. When all the things I want to do and achieve get too much and too overwhelming, and all the fears

creep in (what if I fail, what if I succeed, what will they think of me, and so on), that's when I retreat and shut the world out. I don't pick up the phone, don't respond to emails, miss the opportunities and appointments, and so on. It's not a good place to be in. I'm the queen of procrastination and often leave everything until the last minute, and feel horribly guilty in the process for not doing enough. But I have learned that I do work best on a tight deadline anyway (when there's no room to overthink things to death!), so I'm slowly accepting that fact and giving myself some slack. Awhile back I heard Aaron Sorkin say that often for him the process of writing involves lying on the sofa and looking at the ceiling, or doing something completely unrelated, while his brain is hard at work thinking up ideas or processing information. That gave me permission to accept that sometimes that's exactly what it'll look like in my world too, and it doesn't mean that there's no progress. Still, procrastination means that long-term personal projects that don't have a deadline as such don't get completed (or get abandoned halfway through), and that stifles my progress as a creative."

TIPS:
- Start super small. Break one task into smaller chunks. Plant the first seed.
- If it will take less than five minutes, do it straight away.
- If you can, avoid checking your phone first thing in the morning and see what you can get done before checking.
- Listen to some music that you know makes you feel motivated.

3. THE INNER CRITIC

Negative self-talk seems to be the biggest culprit here. If we can work on quieting that voice, that inner bully, then everything else can then follow more easily. Selina Barker calls these negative voices "the shitty committee," which always makes me laugh. I have always had a self-loathing voice that interrupts a positive flow of thoughts. A distraction from a moment of happiness, that voice will sneak in and pepper my brain with questions: *But did you really deserve that? Does that person really like you? Things might be good now, but remember, things are probably going to go downhill soon.*

Sometimes, something just clicks into place and you understand how easy it could be to just . . . stop. Now, when I catch my inner critic about to drag myself down, I cut myself off. I will not finish my sentence. It's taken awhile to retrain myself to stop doing it, but I decided that I already had a master's degree in negative self-talk, I'd gotten the trophy, and I didn't need to do it anymore.

So, if building a less shakable confidence and stronger sense of self-worth plays a key role in reducing our tendencies to self-sabotage, then we need actionable ways to build ourselves up and tools to help us be kinder to ourselves. If I look back at my own moments of self-sabotage, every single one could have been nipped in the bud if my self-worth was riding high that day. Strong self-worth says no to toxic people reentering your life, it stops you reading negative comments about your work, it chooses enough rest, it dumps the bad boyfriend, it makes you a good listener, it encourages you to ask the people who love you for help. Self-worth ultimately quiets that inner critic. The more we are comfortable in our own skin, the less we will judge ourselves—and others.

I always find comfort in something my friend Lucy Sheridan has said to me: "If you can think and feel your way into a problem, then you can think and feel your way out again." Our reality really does live inside our minds, and the life we live very much depends on how we talk to ourselves. Criticizing ourselves isn't just a casual thing we do; it can actually affect the future life we are trying to create.

As writer and therapist Andrea Glik says, "Instead of: It's bad (I'm bad) that I need drugs/alcohol/extreme coping to feel better. Try: It's extremely resourceful that my nervous system has found something to regulate itself. I wonder what else I could utilize that's inside myself and would make me feel better in the long run?" What can we utilize that's inside ourselves?

Rebecca Cunningham, 31, dentist

> "I am an enthusiastic and hard worker, I would
> like to believe, but often the lack of support or the
> unnecessary questioning by those around me can
> cause feelings of self-questioning and lowering
> of self-esteem, even when I know I am doing my
> job to the best of my ability, professionally and
> ethically. This environmental atmosphere can
> lead to immense self-stress. I'm a harsh critic to
> myself, and the positivity is stifled when there is a
> lack of external support to appease the self-critic.
> Things I say to myself: Is that good enough?
> Clarified enough? I thought I was pretty clear
> on my thoughts, processes, and justifications,
> so why am I having to justify myself? Is what I'm

saying not reasonable? The explanatory ramble that I often go on feels like an internal friction burn. Like a cramp no one can see."

TIP: A tip from Dr. Soph is to personalize and externalize your inner critic.

- Think about your inner critic. Give it a name, a form, a voice.
- Think about whom your inner critic represents, whether the language of the inner critic sounds like someone from your past (as the inner critic often uses the language of someone critical in your life).
- Create stock responses you can use when your inner critic arises, like, "Thank you, *insert inner critic's name here.* I see you and I hear you. I know you are trying to protect me in your own way, but I've got this. I am OK."
- Or . . . think of whether you would think it was OK to say your inner critic's words to a friend who was in your situation. If the answer is no, think of a specific friend, and then think of what you would say to them if they were in your situation.

4. FEAR OF SELF-PROMOTION

I have noticed that many creatives don't necessarily struggle with creating their work but the idea of promoting it to the world. There used to be more traditional ways of promoting work: A label might market your music for you or an art gallery might show your paintings. But then, along came social media. And now, as we live and move in an increasingly digital landscape, we have to be more of our own mouthpiece. We have to shout about our own work or get drowned out by the noise. As the old saying goes: Nobody is going to find you on the third page of Google. You have to put your work out there, however painful or awkward it might be at first.

Hayley Dean, 27, TV production

> "I believe it's directly linked to imposter syndrome. I get really scared to market myself as a specific 'thing' in case someone calls me out on it or feels that I don't have the validation to label myself in that way. For example, someone recently referred to me as a 'freelance filmmaker' and I was like, 'Oh no, that's not what I do; I

freelance in the film/TV industry.' They looked at me confused and queried, 'Yes, but didn't you just make a promo film for XYZ?' and they aren't wrong, but I'll always reply desperate to rid myself of a label I don't feel I've earned or deserve—'Well, yes, but, erm, that's just because I met them at my old job and then they got in contact and asked if I'd be interested. It's not what I usually do. I'm not very good.' Naturally, a conversation like that would happen more in a social setting and I can force myself to alter my response in a professional environment, particularly when presented with a potential work opportunity. I think it's because I always believe there is someone more qualified or advanced who could do the job, so it's my way of justifying my awareness of that. What I fail to remember is that they know what I've done previously, have seen examples, and if they wanted to hire Steven Spielberg, then they would, but their budget is more geared toward me and what I can offer. But from the way I struggle and panic, you would think I submitted Spielberg's résumé and tried to pass it off as my own!"

TIP: Practice self-promoting to your friends. Tell them about the work you're doing and why you're proud of it. Then practice writing that Instagram caption or LinkedIn post in this same tone of voice. Realize that self-promoting is not an ego move; it is a business move. If you tell people about your work, you'll probably get more work.

WHO TOLD YOU THAT?

I can't cook. So I'm told. I don't really think it's true, but it's become a sort of identity cloak I've put on based on other people's comments over the years. At school, I admit I found Home Ec cooking classes really boring. In class I would mess around with my friends, and once I "washed" some cakes because I put too much flour on them. Yes, I know, you do not wash cakes. It's a mishap that's stayed with me my entire adult life. I'll say something as innocent as "I'm off now," and one of my friends from school will reply, "To wash some cakes?" It's funny, but it's annoying because I've never been able to overcome this label given to me in my youth. I actually really enjoy cooking now. But sadly, I am still treated as the Bridget Jones of the group who makes blue soup at a dinner party. I could make the most amazing five-star, six-course gourmet dinner and I'd still be known as the woman who once washed a cake. You are allowed to reinvent yourself as an adult and unpick some of those labels that were stuck onto you. Of course, it's funny and I can laugh now: But adhering to old labels and slipping back into old habits can sabotage your future progress. It's about gradually outgrowing these moments of being teased, even just in your own mind so that you can grow into your current, ever-changing skin.

WRITE DOWN THE ANSWERS TO THESE QUESTIONS:

- What is something you were once told about yourself that you still believe?
- Think of something you think you're bad at. Ask yourself who told you that. Where did that idea come from?
- Is it true anymore?
- What do you believe is true about yourself now?
- Try doing the thing you think you are bad at more regularly and integrate it into your life as much as you can. Practice makes perfect. Dispel the myth to yourself and to others.

TIME TO MAKE A CHANGE

SO, HOW DO YOU STOP SELF-SABOTAGING ONCE YOU
recognize that's what you're doing? Of course, the most
human thing to do would be to go into a "shame spiral,"
as Brené Brown calls it, or just sweep it under the rug
altogether. Even asking friends or family for solutions
doesn't always work, as they are often inclined to give
you a hug and say: "Oh, you'll be fine!" Of course,
sometimes, that can be exactly what we need—but what
do the experts think?

I asked Dr. Jessamy Hibberd for her opinion. What
should we do when we first recognize self-sabotaging
behavior? She suggests starting with forgiveness. "It is
much better to use compassion in these situations and to
recognize what it means to be human. Sabotage is linked

to negative feelings, so if you reduce these through forgiveness, it puts you in a better position to do well next time." It seems that having some empathy and kindness toward ourselves is at the heart of reducing our sabotaging behavior.

I also spoke with professor of human brain research Vincent Walsh, who took an optimistic view of things: "We all make bad decisions from time to time. We do things badly, we get lazy, we take the easy way out . . . but we rarely screw ourselves over." He said that human beings are extremely resilient, something we can forget when we are deep in self-sabotage mode. "We tend to survive and persevere in spite of things." So perhaps even beyond forgiveness, we actually deserve some credit.

I was looking for a brutal diagnosis, confirmation that my self-sabotage was proof of some terrible flaw, but I wasn't going to get one. Instead, I was given compassion and understanding as a way to fix things. The *New York Times* recently published a piece titled "When Did Self-Help Become Self-Care?" that explored how the cult of wellness has taken over the self-help industry. "On Instagram, the axis of millennial life, there are about two million posts tagged #selfhelp, while there are around 18 million for #selfcare."

I am a fan of self-care, but I am a bigger fan of practical advice. As Professor Walsh says, it helps to have a mixture of "you're only human" *and* an element of "suck it up!" Self-compassion is vital, but so is self-determination. Comforting phrases are nice, and so are Himalayan bath salts and lavender oil, but at some point, we have to draw our own line in the sand and say: *Enough is enough.*

Inspired by my conversation with Professor Walsh, here are some tips on how to track any self-sabotaging behavior. We can't expect a magic pill or a shiny button to press, but we can make small, manageable changes if we want to:

1. **IF YOU WANT TO MAKE ACTUAL CHANGE, THEN TAKE IT SERIOUSLY.** Professor Walsh recommends keeping a notebook or measuring your progress in some way so you can actually evaluate your behavior. There often isn't any urgent pressure to optimize or improve our lives. If we want to quit our job, or eat differently, or go to therapy, no one will force us to do so. Change must come from within. Making change takes courage and commitment from ourselves.

2. **TAKE RESPONSIBILITY FOR YOUR BEHAVIOR.** The "fundamental attribution error" is one of the most important concepts in psychology. We make up external excuses for our behavior all the time. We look at other people and think, "You didn't meet your

deadline? Well, you're unreliable." But if *we* didn't meet our deadline, then we can justify it to ourselves: "Well, my boiler, my workload, my aunt got sick, etc." We need to face the music, basically.

3. **STOP LOOKING FOR QUICK OR MAGIC ANSWERS.** Everything worthwhile takes a ton of hard work; there is no such thing as overnight success. I recently read Farrah Storr's *The Discomfort Zone,* which argues that in order to truly thrive we have to get uncomfortable. In a world that pushes self-care to the point of coddling, it's important to remember that sometimes you have to be challenged, and challenge is not always fun. Nothing in life is an insurmountable challenge, only a series of small, uncomfortable tests that can be overcome.

4. **LET SOME THINGS GO.** The "sunk cost error"—also sometimes called "the sunk cost fallacy"—is when we have made a bad investment (in money or time or emotion) and we keep investing more because we've "put too much into it to let it fail now." At the end of the day, we have to let some things go. It doesn't mean we are a failure, just that a thing we tried didn't quite work, and that's OK.

CHOOSE SELF-WORTH OVER SELF-SABOTAGE

It makes sense to me now why we must try to internalize our accomplishments as much as we can. We must believe our good qualities are fact and not fiction. We must truly inhale what's great and true about ourselves and use it as oxygen. We must learn not to solely rely on inconsistent external validation in order to breathe in this world and survive. What I've learned is that my self-sabotage behavior also manifests itself in me wanting a reaction or wanting attention. Writing this book about self-sabotage has been a lesson in reminding me that we should get to know ourselves really well. Give ourselves the attention we deserve. Be aware of our triggers and the things that make us react. Every time we ignore our intuition, we are letting self-sabotage in.

We all deserve endless opportunities to thrive and be happy and the tools to actually let success into our lives. Here are some tips, compiled with the help of Dr. Jessamy Hibberd, for tackling your confidence issues head-on:

1. **RECOGNIZE THAT HAVING CONFIDENCE IS A GOOD THING.** Talking about the things you are proud of is something we should all be doing with the people we care about. People who care about you will want to hear about and share in your success! Doing this will normalize it and make you more comfortable with your success.

2. **INTERNALIZE YOUR SUCCESSES.** Recognizing and embracing your successes gives you a fuller picture of your life—rather than focusing on the bits you're unhappy with. Praise and positive feedback are great in the moment, but we need to be able to internalize them so we build an inner measure of how we're doing.

3. **KEEP TRACK OF ALL YOUR ACHIEVEMENTS AND CELEBRATE THE LITTLE THINGS NO MATTER HOW SMALL.** Take compliments on board. Stop minimizing achievements. Record your role in making things happen. Accept praise without qualification.

4. **DON'T WAIT UNTIL YOU FEEL LIKE DOING SOMETHING TO DO IT.** The best thing is to just get started. Even if you don't feel inspired, you can still make progress.

5. **GET IN TOUCH WITH YOUR FUTURE SELF.** Make sure you're really clear about why you want to do what you're doing. How will it make things better for you in the future? Why will you benefit? Make your goals concrete and think about what you'll gain if you reach them. Your future self will thank you.

YOU DO DESERVE TO BE HAPPY

YOU ARE ALLOWED TO FALL IN LOVE WITH YOUR OWN
life. It can be just as easy to recognize the good in our own
lives as it is to recognize the good in others'. Our brains
have the power to reshape our perception and change our
thinking patterns and therefore can change our lives too.
We can't control the outside world, but we can control what
goes on within us. What if we—*inside of ourselves*—get to
be our own happy place?

I dare you to accept the next good thing—accept the
compliment, accept the offer, accept the opportunity—
without trying to justify why you don't deserve it or how it
could all go wrong. Yes, it is only natural to ask, what if it
all goes wrong?

But you must also ask yourself: What if it goes right?

ACKNOWLEDGMENTS

THANK YOU TO JP AT THE POUND PROJECT FOR GIVING me the space to explore the subject of self-sabotage for the first time in our first, crowdfunded edition of this book.

Huge thank-you to Allison Adler and my Andrews McMeel publishing family for the opportunity to expand on the subject and bring the book to a wider readership.

To my agent, Abigail Bergstrom, for being wonderful, as always.

Thank you to everyone who spoke to me about self-sabotage for the book.

Writing this book helped me get on the right path to beating my own self-sabotage, and I hope it may do the same for you.

ABOUT THE AUTHOR

EMMA GANNON is the author of *The Multi-Hyphen Life* and *Olive*. She is an award-winning podcaster, speaker, and columnist who has been published everywhere from the *Times* (UK) to *Teen Vogue*. Her popular interview podcast, *Ctrl Alt Delete,* where she discusses work, culture, and careers with interesting people from all walks of life, has been nominated for a Webby Award and has been recommended by *Wired, Esquire, Elle, Red, Marie Claire,* and many more. She lives in London.

Enjoy *Sabotage* as an audiobook narrated by the author, wherever audiobooks are sold.

Andrews McMeel Publishing
a division of Andrews McMeel Universal
1130 Walnut Street, Kansas City, Missouri 64106

www.andrewsmcmeel.com

20 21 22 23 24 BVG 10 9 8 7 6 5 4 3 2 1

ISBN: 978-1-5248-6241-1

Library of Congress Control Number: 2020938304

Editor: Allison Adler
Art Director: Diane Marsh
Production Editor: Elizabeth A. Garcia
Production Manager: Cliff Koehler

ATTENTION: SCHOOLS AND BUSINESSES
Andrews McMeel books are available at quantity discounts with
bulk purchase for educational, business, or sales promotional use.
For information, please e-mail the Andrews McMeel Publishing
Special Sales Department: specialsales@amuniversal.com.